The Original and #1 Brand Slow Cooker

Family Favorites

Publications International Ltd.

Favorite Brand Name Recipes at www.fbnr.com

Pictured on the front cover: Chicken Fiesta Soup (*page 68*).

Pictured on the back cover (clockwise from upper left): Cherry Flan (*page 52)*, Barbecued Pulled Pork Sandwiches (*page 73*), and Korean BBQ Beef Short Ribs (*page 34*).

ISBN-13: 978-1-4127-2934-5
ISBN-10: 1-4127-2934-3

Manufactured in China.

8 7 6 5 4 3 2 1

Preparation/Cooking Times: Preparation times are based on the approximate amount of time required to assemble the recipe before cooking, baking, chilling, or serving. These times include preparation steps such as measuring, chopping, and mixing. The fact that some preparations and cooking can be done simultaneously is taken into account. Preparation of optional ingredients and serving suggestions is not included.

Table of Contents

16

58

70

STIRRING

Due to the nature of the **CROCK·POT**® slow cooker, there is no need to stir the food unless it specifically says to in your recipe. In fact, taking the lid off to stir food causes the **CROCK·POT**® slow cooker to lose a significant amount of heat, extending the cooking time required. Therefore, it is best not to remove the lid for stirring.

COOKING TEMPERATURES AND FOOD SAFETY

Cooking meats in your **CROCK·POT**® slow cooker is perfectly safe. According to the U.S. Department of Agriculture, bacteria in food is killed at a temperature of 165°F. Meats cooked in the **CROCK·POT**® slow cooker reach an internal temperature in excess of 170°F for beef and as high as 209°F for poultry. It is important to follow the recommended cooking times and to keep the cover on your **CROCK·POT**® slow cooker during the cooking process.

If your food isn't done after 8 hours when the recipe calls for 8 to 10 hours, this could be due to a difference in altitude or to extreme humidity. It also could be due to voltage variations, which are commonplace. Slight fluctuations in power do not have a noticeable effect on most appliances; however, they can slightly alter the cooking times. Allow plenty of time, and remember: It is practically impossible to overcook foods in a **CROCK·POT**® slow cooker. You will learn through experience whether to decrease or increase cooking times.

REMOVABLE STONEWARE

The removable stoneware in your **CROCK·POT**® slow cooker makes cleaning easy. Here are some tips on the use of your stoneware:

● Your **CROCK·POT**® slow cooker makes a great server for hot beverages, appetizers, or dips. Keep it on the WARM setting to maintain the proper serving temperature.

• Because all **CROCK-POT**® slow cookers have wrap-around heat, there is no direct heat at the bottom. For best results, always fill the stoneware at least half full to conform to recommended times. Small quantities can still be cooked, but cooking times will be affected.

BROWNING MEAT

Meat cooked in the **CROCK-POT**® slow cooker will not brown as it would if it were cooked in a skillet or oven at high temperatures. For some recipes, it is not necessary to brown meat before slow cooking. If you prefer the flavor and look of browned meat, however, simply brown the meat in a large skillet with nonstick cooking spray before placing it in the stoneware and following the recipe as written.

ADDING INGREDIENTS AT THE END OF THE COOKING TIME

Certain ingredients tend to break down during extended cooking. When possible, add these ingredients toward the end of the cooking time:

● Milk, cream, and sour cream: Add during the last 15 minutes of cooking time.

● Seafood: Add in the last 3 to 15 minutes, depending on the thickness and quantity. Gently stir periodically to ensure even cooking.

COOKING FOR LARGER QUANTITY YIELDS

Follow these guidelines when preparing recipes in a larger unit, such as a 5-, 6-, or 7-quart **CROCK-POT**® slow cooker:

● Roasted meats, chicken, and turkey quantities may be doubled or tripled, but seasonings should be adjusted by no more than half. Flavorful seasonings, such as garlic and chili powder, intensify during long, slow cooking. Add just 25 to 50 percent more spices as needed to balance flavors.

● When preparing a soup or a stew, you may double all ingredients except seasonings (see above), dried herbs, liquids, and thickeners. Increase liquid volume by no more than half or as needed. The **CROCK-POT**® slow cooker lid collects steam, which condenses to keep foods moist and to maintain liquid volume. Do not double thickeners, such as cornstarch, at the beginning. You may always add more thickener later if needed.

● When preparing dishes with beef or pork in a larger unit, such as a 5-, 6-, or 7-quart **CROCK-POT**® slow cooker, browning the meat in a skillet before adding it to the stoneware yields the best results; the meat will cook more evenly.

● When preparing baked goods, it is best not to double or triple the recipe. Simply prepare the original recipe as many times as needed to serve more people.

Impress Your Guests

FABULOUS FARE FOR ALL KINDS OF ENTERTAINING OCCASIONS

Spicy Fruit Dessert

MAKES 4 TO 6 SERVINGS

PREP TIME: 10 TO 15 MINUTES

COOK TIME: 4 TO 6 HOURS (LOW) ■ 2 TO 3 HOURS (HIGH)

¼ cup orange marmalade

¼ teaspoon pumpkin pie spice

1 can (6 ounces) frozen orange juice concentrate

2 cups canned pears, drained and diced

2 cups carambola (star fruit), sliced and seeds removed

1. Combine marmalade, pumpkin pie spice, orange juice concentrate, pears and carambola in **CROCK-POT**® slow cooker.

2. Cover; cook on LOW 4 to 6 hours or on HIGH 2 to 3 hours or until done. Serve warm over pound cake or ice cream.

Fall-Apart Pork Roast

MAKES 6 SERVINGS

PREP TIME: 10 TO 15 MINUTES

COOK TIME: 7 TO 8 HOURS (LOW) ■ 3 TO 4 HOURS (HIGH)

⅔ cup whole almonds

⅔ cup raisins

3 tablespoons vegetable oil, divided

½ cup chopped onion

4 cloves garlic, chopped

2¾ pounds lean boneless pork shoulder roast, well trimmed

1 can (14½ ounces) diced fire-roasted tomatoes *or* diced tomatoes, undrained

1 cup cubed bread, any variety

½ cup chicken broth

2 ounces Mexican chocolate, chopped

2 tablespoons chipotle peppers in adobo sauce, chopped

1 teaspoon salt

Fresh cilantro, coarsely chopped (optional)

1. Heat large skillet over medium-high heat. Add almonds and toast 3 to 4 minutes, stirring frequently, until fragrant. Add raisins. Cook 1 to 2 minutes longer, stirring constantly, until raisins begin to plump. Place half of almond mixture in large mixing bowl. Reserve remaining half for garnish.

2. In same skillet, heat 1 tablespoon oil. Add onions and garlic. Cook 2 to 3 minutes, stirring constantly, until softened. Add to almond mixture; set aside.

3. Heat remaining oil in same skillet. Add pork roast and brown on all sides, about 5 to 7 minutes. Transfer to **CROCK-POT**® slow cooker.

4. Combine tomatoes with juice, bread, broth, chocolate, chipotle peppers and salt with almond mixture. Process mixture in blender, in 2 or 3 batches, until smooth. Pour mixture over pork.

5. Cover; cook on LOW 7 to 8 hours or on HIGH 3 to 4 hours or until pork is done. Remove roast from **CROCK-POT**® slow cooker. Whisk sauce until smooth and spoon over roast. Garnish with reserved almond mixture and chopped cilantro, if desired.

Risotto-Style Peppered Rice

MAKES 4 TO 6 SERVINGS

PREP TIME: 10 TO 15 MINUTES

COOK TIME: 4 TO 5 HOURS (LOW)

- 1 cup uncooked converted long-grain rice
- 1 medium green bell pepper, chopped
- 1 medium red bell pepper, chopped
- 1 cup chopped onion
- ½ teaspoon ground turmeric
- ⅛ teaspoon ground red pepper (optional)
- 1 can (14½ ounces) fat-free chicken broth
- 4 ounces Monterey Jack cheese with jalapeño peppers, cubed
- ½ cup milk
- 4 tablespoons (½ stick) butter, cubed
- 1 teaspoon salt

1. Place rice, bell peppers, onion, turmeric and red pepper, if desired, in **CROCK-POT**® slow cooker. Stir in broth.

2. Cover; cook on LOW 4 to 5 hours or until rice is done. Stir in cheese, milk, butter and salt; fluff rice with fork. Cover; cook on LOW 5 minutes or until cheese melts.

Herbed Fall Vegetables

MAKES 6 SERVINGS

PREP TIME: 10 MINUTES

COOK TIME: 4½ HOURS (LOW) ■ 3 HOURS (HIGH)

- **3** parsnips, peeled and cut into ½-inch dice
- **2** medium Yukon Gold potatoes, peeled and cut into ½-inch dice
- **2** medium sweet potatoes, peeled and cut into ½-inch dice
- **1** medium head fennel, sliced and cut into ½-inch dice
- **½** to ¾ cup chopped fresh herbs, such as tarragon, parsley, sage or thyme
- **4** tablespoons butter (½ stick), cut into small pieces
- **1** cup chicken broth
- **1** tablespoon Dijon mustard
- **1** tablespoon salt
  Freshly ground black pepper to taste

1. Combine parsnips, potatoes, fennel, herbs and butter in **CROCK-POT**® slow cooker.

2. Whisk together broth, mustard, salt and pepper in small bowl. Pour mixture over vegetables.

3. Cook on LOW 4½ hours or on HIGH 3 hours until vegetables are tender, stirring occasionally to ensure even cooking.

Hot Broccoli Cheese Dip

MAKES ABOUT 6 CUPS

PREP TIME: 10 TO 15 MINUTES

COOK TIME: 30 MINUTES TO 1 HOUR (HIGH) PLUS 2 TO 4 HOURS (LOW)

½ cup butter
6 stalks celery, sliced
2 onions, chopped
2 cans (4 ounces each) sliced mushrooms, drained
¼ cup plus 2 tablespoons all-purpose flour
2 cans (10¾ ounces each) condensed cream of celery soup
5 to 6 ounces garlic cheese, cut into cubes
2 packages (10 ounces each) frozen broccoli spears
French bread slices, bell pepper strips, cherry tomatoes

1. Melt butter in large skillet. Add celery, onion and mushrooms; cook and stir until translucent. Stir in flour and cook 2 to 3 minutes. Transfer to **CROCK-POT**® slow cooker.

2. Stir in soup, cheese and broccoli. Cover; cook on HIGH, stirring every 15 minutes, until cheese is melted. Turn **CROCK-POT**® slow cooker to LOW. Cover; cook 2 to 4 hours or until ready to serve.

3. Serve warm with bread slices or assorted vegetables, as desired.

Chai Tea

MAKES 8 TO 10 SERVINGS

PREP TIME: 8 MINUTES

COOK TIME: 2 TO 2½ HOURS (HIGH)

- 2 quarts (8 cups) water
- 8 bags black tea
- ¾ cup sugar*
- 16 whole cloves
- 16 whole cardamom seeds, pods removed (optional)
- 5 cinnamon sticks
- 8 slices fresh ginger
- 1 cup milk

***Chai tea is typically a sweet drink. For less sweetness, reduce sugar to ½ cup.**

1. Combine water, tea, sugar, cloves, cardamom, if desired, cinnamon and ginger in **CROCK-POT**® slow cooker. Cover; cook on HIGH 2 to 2½ hours.

2. Strain mixture; discard solids. (At this point, tea may be covered and refrigerated for up to 3 days.)

3. Stir in milk just before serving. Serve warm or chilled.

Turkey with Pecan-Cherry Stuffing

MAKES 8 SERVINGS

PREP TIME: 20 MINUTES

COOK TIME: 5 TO 6 HOURS (LOW)

1 fresh or frozen boneless turkey breast (about 3 to 4 pounds)
2 cups cooked rice
⅓ cup chopped pecans
⅓ cup dried cherries or cranberries
1 teaspoon poultry seasoning
¼ cup peach, apricot or plum preserves
1 teaspoon Worcestershire sauce

1. Thaw turkey breast, if frozen. Remove and discard skin. Cut slices ¾ of the way through turkey at 1-inch intervals.

2. Stir together rice, pecans, cherries and poultry seasoning in large bowl. Stuff rice mixture between slices. If needed, skewer turkey lengthwise to hold together.

3. Place turkey in **CROCK-POT**® slow cooker. Cover; cook on LOW 5 to 6 hours or until turkey registers 170°F on meat thermometer inserted into thickest part of breast, not touching stuffing.

4. Stir together preserves and Worcestershire sauce. Spoon over turkey. Cover; let stand 5 minutes. Remove skewer before serving.

Stuffed Chicken Breasts

MAKES 6 SERVINGS

PREP TIME: 20 MINUTES

COOK TIME: 5½ TO 6 HOURS (LOW) ■ 4 HOURS (HIGH)

 6 boneless skinless chicken breasts
 8 ounces feta cheese, crumbled
 3 cups chopped fresh spinach leaves
 ⅓ cup oil-packed sun-dried tomatoes, drained and chopped
 1 teaspoon minced lemon peel
 1 teaspoon dried basil, oregano or mint
 ½ teaspoon garlic powder
    Freshly ground black pepper, to taste
 1 can (15 ounces) diced tomatoes, undrained
 ½ cup oil-cured olives*
    Hot cooked polenta

*If using pitted olives, add to CROCK-POT® slow cooker in final hour of cooking.

1. Place chicken breast between 2 pieces of plastic wrap. Using tenderizer mallet or back of skillet, pound chicken until about ¼ inch thick. Repeat with remaining chicken.

2. Combine feta, spinach, sun-dried tomatoes, lemon peel, basil, garlic powder and pepper in medium bowl.

3. Lay pounded chicken, smooth side down, on work surface. Place approximately 2 tablespoons feta mixture on wide end of chicken. Roll tightly. Repeat with remaining chicken.

4. Place rolled chicken, seam side down, in **CROCK-POT®** slow cooker. Top with diced tomatoes with juice and olives.

5. Cover; cook on LOW 5½ to 6 hours or on HIGH 4 hours. Serve with polenta.

Maple-Glazed Meatballs

MAKES ABOUT 48 MEATBALLS

PREP TIME: 10 MINUTES

COOK TIME: 5 TO 6 HOURS (LOW)

1½ cups ketchup
1   cup maple syrup or maple-flavored syrup
⅓   cup reduced-sodium soy sauce
1   tablespoon quick-cooking tapioca
1½ teaspoons ground allspice
1   teaspoon dry mustard
2   packages (about 16 ounces each) frozen fully cooked meatballs, partially thawed and separated
1   can (20 ounces) pineapple chunks in juice, drained

1. Combine ketchup, maple syrup, soy sauce, tapioca, allspice and mustard in **CROCK-POT**® slow cooker. Carefully stir meatballs and pineapple chunks into ketchup mixture.

2. Cover; cook on LOW 5 to 6 hours. Stir before serving. Insert cocktail picks to serve.

Poached Pears with Raspberry Sauce

MAKES 4 TO 5 SERVINGS

PREP TIME: 20 MINUTES

COOK TIME: 3½ TO 4 HOURS (LOW)

- 4 cups cran-raspberry juice cocktail
- 2 cups Rhine or Riesling wine, or other sweet white wine
- ¼ cup sugar
- 2 cinnamon sticks, broken into halves
- 4 to 5 firm Bosc or Anjou pears, peeled and cored
- 1 package (10 ounces) frozen raspberries in syrup, thawed
  Fresh berries (optional)

1. Combine juice, wine, sugar and cinnamon in **CROCK-POT**® slow cooker. Immerse pears in liquid. Cover; cook on LOW 3½ to 4 hours or until pears are tender. Remove pears and discard cinnamon sticks.

2. Process raspberries in food processor or blender until smooth; strain and discard seeds. Spoon raspberry sauce onto serving plates; place pears on top of sauce. Garnish with fresh berries, if desired.

World-Class Cuisine

FESTIVE RECIPES FROM THE MOST POPULAR CUISINES AROUND THE WORLD

Thai Chicken

MAKES 6 SERVINGS

PREP TIME: 10 TO 15 MINUTES

COOK TIME: 8 TO 9 HOURS (LOW) ■ 3 TO 4 HOURS (HIGH)

2½ pounds chicken pieces
 1 cup hot salsa
 ¼ cup peanut butter
 2 tablespoons lime juice
 1 tablespoon soy sauce
 1 teaspoon minced fresh ginger
    Hot cooked rice
 ½ cup peanuts, chopped
 2 tablespoons chopped fresh cilantro

1. Place chicken in **CROCK-POT**® slow cooker. Mix together salsa, peanut butter, lime juice, soy sauce and ginger; pour over chicken.

2. Cover; cook on LOW 8 to 9 hours or on HIGH 3 to 4 hours or until done.

3. Serve chicken and sauce over rice; sprinkle with peanuts and cilantro.

Best Asian-Style Ribs

MAKES 6 TO 8 SERVINGS

PREP TIME: 10 TO 15 MINUTES

COOK TIME: 6 TO 7 HOURS (LOW) ■ 3 TO 3½ HOURS (HIGH)

2 full racks baby back pork ribs, split into 3 sections each
6 ounces hoisin sauce
2 tablespoons minced fresh ginger
½ cup maraschino cherries
½ cup rice wine vinegar
Water to cover
4 scallions, chopped

1. Combine ribs, hoisin sauce, ginger, cherries, vinegar and water in **CROCK-POT**® slow cooker. Cover; cook on LOW 6 to 7 hours or on HIGH 3 to 3½ hours or until pork is done.

2. Remove ribs. To thicken sauce, heat, uncovered, until consistency of barbecue sauce. Or pour sauce into saucepan; cook to thicken to desired consistency. Sprinkle ribs with scallions. Serve ribs with extra sauce.

Carne Rellenos

MAKES 6 SERVINGS

PREP TIME: 20 MINUTES

COOK TIME: 6 TO 8 HOURS (LOW) ■ 3 TO 4 HOURS (HIGH)

- 1 can (4 ounces) mild whole green chilies, drained
- 4 ounces cream cheese, softened
- 1 flank steak (about 2 pounds)
- 1½ cups salsa verde (green salsa)

1. Slit whole chilies open on one side with sharp knife; stuff with cream cheese.

2. Open steak flat on sheet of waxed paper. Score steak and turn over. Lay stuffed chilies across unscored side of steak. Roll up and tie with kitchen string.

3. Place steak in **CROCK-POT**® slow cooker. Pour in salsa. Cover; cook on LOW 6 to 8 hours or on HIGH 3 to 4 hours or until meat is fork-tender.

4. Remove steak and cut into 6 pieces. Serve with sauce.

Cioppino

MAKES 6 SERVINGS

PREP TIME: 20 TO 30 MINUTES

COOK TIME: 10 TO 12½ HOURS (LOW)

- 1 pound cod, halibut or any firm-fleshed white fish, cubed
- 1 cup mushrooms, sliced
- 2 carrots, sliced
- 1 onion, chopped
- 1 green bell pepper, chopped
- 1 teaspoon minced garlic
- 1 can (15 ounces) tomato sauce
- 1 can (14 ounces) beef broth
- 1 teaspoon salt
- ½ teaspoon black pepper
- ½ teaspoon dried oregano
- 1 can (7 ounces) cooked clams
- ½ pound cooked shrimp
- 1 package (6 ounces) cooked crabmeat
  Minced parsley

1. Combine fish pieces, mushrooms, carrots, onion, bell pepper, garlic, tomato sauce, broth, salt, black pepper and oregano in **CROCK-POT**® slow cooker. Cover; cook on LOW 10 to 12 hours.

2. Turn **CROCK-POT**® slow cooker to HIGH. Add clams, shrimp and crabmeat. Cover; cook 15 to 30 minutes or until seafood is heated through. Garnish with parsley before serving.

Mediterranean Chicken

MAKES 6 SERVINGS

PREP TIME: 15 TO 20 MINUTES

COOK TIME: 8 TO 10 HOURS (LOW) ■ 4 TO 5 HOURS (HIGH)

- 1 tablespoon olive oil
- 2 pounds boneless skinless chicken breasts
- 1 can (28 ounces) diced tomatoes, undrained
- 2 onions, chopped
- ½ cup sherry
- Juice of 2 lemons
- 6 teaspoons minced garlic
- 2 cinnamon sticks
- 1 bay leaf
- ½ teaspoon black pepper
- 1 pound cooked broad noodles
- ½ cup feta cheese

1. Heat oil in large skillet over medium heat until hot. Add chicken and cook to brown both sides, 2 to 3 minutes per side; set aside.

2. Combine tomatoes with juice, onions, sherry, lemon juice, garlic, cinnamon, bay leaf and pepper in **CROCK-POT**® slow cooker. Add chicken. Cover; cook on LOW 8 to 10 hours or on HIGH 4 to 5 hours, or until done.

3. Remove cinnamon sticks and bay leaf. Serve chicken and sauce over cooked noodles. Sprinkle with cheese just before serving.

Caribbean Sweet Potato & Bean Stew

MAKES 4 SERVINGS

PREP TIME: 10 MINUTES

COOK TIME: 5 TO 6 HOURS (LOW)

- 2 medium sweet potatoes (about 1 pound), peeled and cut into 1-inch cubes
- 2 cups frozen cut green beans
- 1 can (15 ounces) black beans, rinsed and drained
- 1 can (14½ ounces) vegetable broth
- 1 small onion, sliced
- 2 teaspoons Caribbean jerk seasoning
- ½ teaspoon dried thyme
- ¼ teaspoon salt
- ¼ teaspoon ground cinnamon
- Salt and black pepper, to taste
- ⅓ cup slivered almonds, toasted*
- Hot pepper sauce (optional)

**To toast almonds, spread in single layer in heavy-bottomed skillet. Cook over medium heat 1 to 2 minutes, stirring frequently, until nuts are lightly browned. Remove from skillet immediately. Cool before using.

1. Combine sweet potatoes, beans, broth, onion, jerk seasoning, thyme, salt and cinnamon in **CROCK-POT**® slow cooker.

2. Cover; cook on LOW 5 to 6 hours or until vegetables are tender.

3. Adjust seasonings. Sprinkle with almonds. Serve with hot sauce, if desired.

Spanish Paella-Style Rice

MAKES 6 SERVINGS

  2   cans (14½ ounces each) chicken broth
1½   cups uncooked converted long-grain rice
  1   small red bell pepper, diced
⅓   cup dry white wine or water
½   teaspoon saffron threads, crushed *or* ½ teaspoon ground turmeric
⅛   teaspoon crushed red pepper flakes
½   cup frozen peas, thawed
      Salt, to taste

1. Combine broth, rice, bell pepper, wine, saffron and pepper flakes in **CROCK-POT**® slow cooker; mix well.

2. Cover; cook on LOW 4 hours or until liquid is absorbed.

3. Stir in peas. Cover; cook 15 to 30 minutes or until peas are hot. Season with salt.

Note: Paella is a Spanish dish of saffron-flavored rice combined with a variety of meats, seafood and vegetables. Paella is traditionally served in a wide, shallow dish.

Variation: Add ½ cup cooked chicken, ham, chorizo or seafood when adding peas.

Korean BBQ Beef Short Ribs

MAKES 6 SERVINGS

PREP TIME: 10 TO 15 MINUTES

COOK TIME: 7 TO 8 HOURS (LOW) ■ 3 TO 4 HOURS (HIGH)

- 4 to 4½ pounds beef short ribs
- ¼ cup chopped green onions with tops
- ¼ cup tamari or soy sauce
- ¼ cup beef broth or water
- 1 tablespoon packed brown sugar
- 2 teaspoons minced fresh ginger
- 2 teaspoons minced garlic
- ½ teaspoon black pepper
- 2 teaspoons Asian sesame oil
  Hot cooked rice or linguine pasta
- 2 teaspoons sesame seeds, toasted

1. Place ribs in **CROCK·POT**® slow cooker. Combine green onions, soy sauce, broth, brown sugar, ginger, garlic and pepper in medium bowl; mix well and pour over ribs. Cover; cook on LOW 7 to 8 hours or on HIGH 3 to 4 hours or until ribs are fork-tender.

2. Remove ribs from cooking liquid; cool slightly. Trim and discard excess fat. Cut rib meat into bite-size pieces, discarding bones and fat.

3. Let cooking liquid stand 5 minutes to allow fat to rise. Skim off fat and discard.

4. Stir sesame oil into liquid. Return beef to **CROCK·POT**® slow cooker. Cover and cook on LOW 15 to 30 minutes or until mixture is hot. Serve with rice or pasta and garnish with sesame seeds.

Variation: Substitute 3 pounds boneless short ribs for beef short ribs.

Risi Bisi

MAKES 6 SERVINGS

PREP TIME: 15 MINUTES

COOK TIME: 3 TO 4 HOURS (LOW)

1½ cups converted long-grain white rice
¾ cup chopped onion
2 cloves garlic, minced
2 cans (14½ ounces each) reduced-sodium chicken broth
⅓ cup water
¾ teaspoon Italian seasoning
½ teaspoon dried basil
½ cup frozen peas, thawed
¼ cup grated Parmesan cheese
¼ cup toasted pine nuts (optional)

1. Combine rice, onion and garlic in **CROCK-POT**® slow cooker. Bring broth and water to a boil in small saucepan. Stir boiling liquid, Italian seasoning and basil into rice mixture. Cover; cook on LOW 2 to 3 hours or until liquid is absorbed.

2. Add peas. Cover; cook 1 hour. Stir in cheese. Spoon rice into serving bowl. Sprinkle with pine nuts, if desired.

Moroccan Chicken Tagine

MAKES 4 TO 6 SERVINGS

PREP TIME: 30 TO 45 MINUTES

COOK TIME: 4 TO 5 HOURS (LOW)

- 3 pounds chicken pieces, skin removed
- 2 cups chicken broth
- 1 can (14½ ounces) diced tomatoes, undrained
- 2 onions, chopped
- 1 cup dried apricots, chopped
- 4 cloves garlic, minced
- 2 teaspoons ground cumin
- 1 teaspoon ground cinnamon
- 1 teaspoon ground ginger
- ½ teaspoon ground coriander
- ½ teaspoon ground red pepper
- 6 sprigs fresh cilantro
- 1 tablespoon cornstarch
- 1 tablespoon water
- 1 can (15 ounces) garbanzo beans, rinsed and drained
- 2 tablespoons chopped fresh cilantro
- ¼ cup slivered almonds, toasted*
  Hot cooked couscous or rice

*To toast almonds, spread in single layer in heavy-bottomed skillet. Cook over medium heat 1 to 2 minutes, stirring frequently, until nuts are lightly browned. Remove from skillet immediately. Cool before using.

1. Place chicken in **CROCK-POT**® slow cooker. Combine broth, tomatoes with juice, onions, apricots, garlic, cumin, cinnamon, ginger, coriander, red pepper and cilantro in medium bowl; pour over chicken.

2. Cover; cook on LOW 4 to 5 hours or until chicken is no longer pink in center. Transfer chicken to serving platter; cover to keep warm.

3. Combine cornstarch and water in small bowl; mix until smooth. Stir cornstarch mixture and beans into **CROCK-POT**® slow cooker. Cover; cook on HIGH 15 minutes or until sauce is thickened. Pour sauce over chicken. Sprinkle with cilantro and toasted almonds. Serve with couscous.

Spectacular Sides

APPEALING ACCOMPANIMENTS FOR MEALTIME VARIETY

Spinach Gorgonzola Corn Bread

MAKES 10 TO 12 SERVINGS

PREP TIME: 8 MINUTES

COOK TIME: 1½ HOURS (HIGH)

2	boxes (8½ ounces each) corn bread mix
3	eggs
½	cup cream
1	box (10 ounces) frozen chopped spinach, thawed and drained
1	cup crumbled Gorgonzola cheese
1	teaspoon ground black pepper
	Paprika (optional)

Coat **CROCK-POT**® slow cooker with nonstick cooking spray. Mix all ingredients in medium bowl. Pour batter into **CROCK-POT**® slow cooker. Cover; cook on HIGH 1½ hours. Sprinkle top with paprika for more colorful crust, if desired. Let bread cool completely before inverting onto serving platter.

Note: Cook only on HIGH setting for proper crust and texture.

Creamy Curried Spinach

MAKES 6 TO 8 SERVINGS

PREP TIME: 10 TO 15 MINUTES

COOK TIME: 3 TO 4 HOURS (LOW) ■ 2 HOURS (HIGH)

- 3 packages (10 ounces each) frozen spinach, thawed
- 1 onion, chopped
- 4 teaspoons minced garlic
- 2 tablespoons curry powder
- 2 tablespoons butter, melted
- ¼ cup chicken broth
- ¼ cup heavy cream
- 1 teaspoon lemon juice

Combine spinach, onion, garlic, curry powder, butter and broth in
CROCK-POT® slow cooker. Cover; cook on LOW 3 to 4 hours or on HIGH
2 hours, or until done. Stir in cream and lemon juice 30 minutes before end
of cooking time.

Supper Squash Medley

MAKES 8 TO 10 SERVINGS

PREP TIME: 15 TO 20 MINUTES

COOK TIME: 6½ HOURS (LOW)

- 2 butternut squash, peeled, seeded and diced
- 1 can (28 ounces) tomatoes, undrained
- 1 can (15 ounces) corn, drained
- 2 onions, chopped
- 2 teaspoons minced garlic
- 2 green chilies, chopped
- 2 green bell peppers, chopped
- 1 cup chicken broth
- 1 teaspoon salt
- ½ teaspoon black pepper
- 1 can (6 ounces) tomato paste

1. Combine squash, tomatoes with juice, corn, onions, garlic, chilies, bell peppers, broth, salt and black pepper in **CROCK-POT**® slow cooker. Cover; cook on LOW 6 hours.

2. Remove about ½ cup cooking liquid and blend with tomato paste. Add back to **CROCK-POT**® slow cooker and stir well. Cook 30 minutes or until slightly thickened and heated through.

Caponata

MAKES ABOUT 5 SERVINGS

PREP TIME: 20 TO 25 MINUTES

COOK TIME: 7 TO 8 HOURS (LOW)

1 medium eggplant (about 1 pound), peeled and cut into ½-inch pieces
1 can (14½ ounces) diced Italian plum tomatoes, undrained
1 medium onion, chopped
1 red bell pepper, cut into ½-inch pieces
½ cup medium-hot salsa
¼ cup extra-virgin olive oil
2 tablespoons capers, drained
2 tablespoons balsamic vinegar
3 cloves garlic, minced
1 teaspoon dried oregano
¼ teaspoon salt
⅓ cup packed fresh basil, cut into thin strips
Toasted sliced Italian or French bread

1. Mix eggplant, tomatoes with juice, onion, bell pepper, salsa, oil, capers, vinegar, garlic, oregano and salt in **CROCK-POT**® slow cooker.

2. Cover; cook on LOW 7 to 8 hours or until vegetables are crisp-tender.

3. Stir in basil. Serve at room temperature on toasted bread.

HELPFUL HINTS

When using the **CROCK-POT**® slow cooker, fresh herbs are best added during the last 15 minutes of cooking time. This helps them retain their flavor and vibrant color.

One other spice note to remember: When slow cooking, you may want to use whole herbs and spices rather than crushed or ground. The flavor and aroma of crushed or ground spices may lessen during the extended cooking time. Be sure to taste and adjust seasonings before serving.

Southwestern Corn and Beans

MAKES 6 SERVINGS

PREP TIME: 15 MINUTES

COOK TIME: 7 TO 8 HOURS (LOW) ■ 2 TO 3 HOURS (HIGH)

- 1 tablespoon olive oil
- 1 large onion, diced
- 1 or 2 jalapeño peppers,* diced
- 1 clove garlic, minced
- 2 cans (15 ounces) light red kidney beans, rinsed and drained
- 1 bag (16 ounces) frozen corn, thawed
- 1 can (14½ ounces) diced tomatoes, undrained
- 1 green bell pepper, cut into 1-inch pieces
- 2 teaspoons medium-hot chili powder
- ¾ teaspoon salt
- ½ teaspoon ground cumin
- ½ teaspoon black pepper
  Sour cream or plain yogurt (optional)
  Sliced black olives (optional)

*Jalapeño peppers can sting and irritate the skin; wear rubber gloves when handling peppers and do not touch eyes. Wash hands after handling.

1. Heat oil in medium skillet over medium heat. Add onion, jalapeño and garlic; cook 5 minutes. Add onion mixture, kidney beans, corn, tomatoes with juice, bell pepper, chili powder, salt, cumin and black pepper to **CROCK-POT**® slow cooker; mix well.

2. Cover; cook on LOW 7 to 8 hours or on HIGH 2 to 3 hours or until done.

3. Serve with sour cream and black olives, if desired.

Serving suggestion: For a party, spoon this colorful vegetarian dish into hollowed-out bell peppers or bread bowls.

Orange-Spiced Sweet Potatoes

MAKES 8 SERVINGS

PREP TIME: 10 TO 15 MINUTES

COOK TIME: 4 HOURS (LOW) ■ 2 HOURS (HIGH)

- **2** pounds sweet potatoes, peeled and diced
- **½** cup packed dark brown sugar
- **½** cup butter (1 stick), cut into small pieces
- **1** teaspoon ground cinnamon
- **½** teaspoon ground nutmeg
- **½** teaspoon grated orange peel
- Juice of 1 medium orange
- **¼** teaspoon salt
- **1** teaspoon vanilla
- Chopped toasted pecans (optional)

Place sweet potatoes, brown sugar, butter, cinnamon, nutmeg, orange peel, orange juice, salt and vanilla in **CROCK-POT**® slow cooker. Cover; cook on LOW 4 hours or on HIGH 2 hours, or until potatoes are tender. Sprinkle with pecans before serving, if desired.

Variation: Mash potatoes; add ¼ cup milk or whipping cream. Sprinkle with a mixture of sugar and cinnamon.

Vegetable Curry

MAKES 6 SERVINGS

PREP TIME: 10 TO 15 MINUTES

COOK TIME: 8 TO 9 HOURS (LOW)

- 4   potatoes, diced
- 1   onion, chopped
- 1   red bell pepper, chopped
- 2   carrots, diced
- 2   tomatoes, chopped
- 1   can (6 ounces) tomato paste
- ¾   cup water
- 2   teaspoons cumin seeds
- ½   teaspoon garlic powder
- ½   teaspoon salt
- 3   cups cauliflower florets
- 1   package (10 ounces) frozen peas, thawed

Combine potatoes, onion, bell pepper, carrots and tomatoes in
CROCK-POT® slow cooker. Stir in tomato paste, water, cumin seeds,
garlic powder and salt. Add cauliflower; stir well. Cover; cook on LOW
8 to 9 hours or until vegetables are tender. Stir in peas before serving.

Scalloped Potatoes and Parsnips

MAKES 4 TO 6 SERVINGS

PREP TIME: 15 TO 20 MINUTES

COOK TIME: 7 HOURS (LOW) ■ 3½ HOURS (HIGH)

- 6 tablespoons unsalted butter
- 3 tablespoons all-purpose flour
- 1¾ cups heavy cream
- 2 teaspoons dry mustard
- 1½ teaspoons salt
- 1 teaspoon dried thyme
- ½ teaspoon black pepper
- 2 baking potatoes, peeled, cut in half lengthwise, then cut into ¼-inch slices crosswise
- 2 parsnips, peeled and cut into ¼-inch slices
- 1 onion, chopped
- 2 cups (8 ounces) shredded sharp Cheddar cheese

1. For cream sauce: Melt butter in medium saucepan over medium-high heat. Whisk in flour. Cook and stir 1 to 2 minutes. Slowly whisk in cream, mustard, salt, thyme and pepper. Stir until smooth.

2. Place potatoes, parsnips and onion in **CROCK-POT®** slow cooker. Add cream sauce. Cover; cook on LOW 7 hours or on HIGH 3½ hours, or until potatoes are tender.

3. Stir in cheese. Cover; let stand until cheese melts.

Corn on the Cob with Garlic Herb Butter

MAKES 4 TO 5 SERVINGS

PREP TIME: 10 TO 15 MINUTES

COOK TIME: 4 TO 5 HOURS (LOW) ■ 2 TO 2½ HOURS (HIGH)

½ cup (1 stick) unsalted butter, at room temperature
3 to 4 cloves garlic, minced
2 tablespoons finely minced fresh parsley
4 to 5 ears of corn, husked
Salt and black pepper, to taste

1. Thoroughly mix butter, garlic and parsley in small bowl.

2. Place each ear of corn on a piece of foil and generously spread on butter. Season corn with salt and pepper and tightly seal foil. Place corn in **CROCK-POT**® slow cooker; overlap ears, if necessary. Add enough water to come ¼ of the way up each ear.

3. Cover; cook on LOW 4 to 5 hours or on HIGH 2 to 2½ hours, or until done.

Red Cabbage and Apples

MAKES 4 TO 6 SERVINGS

PREP TIME: 15 TO 20 MINUTES

COOK TIME: 6 HOURS (HIGH)

1   small head red cabbage, cored and thinly sliced
3   medium apples, peeled and grated
¼   cup sugar
½   cup red wine vinegar
1   teaspoon ground cloves
1   cup crisp-cooked and crumbled bacon (optional)
    Fresh apple slices (optional)

Combine cabbage, grated apples, sugar, vinegar and cloves in **CROCK-POT**® slow cooker. Cover; cook on HIGH 6 hours, stirring after 3 hours. To serve, sprinkle with bacon and garnish with apple slices, if desired.

Winter Squash and Apples

MAKES 4 TO 6 SERVINGS

PREP TIME: 15 MINUTES

COOK TIME: 6 TO 7 HOURS (LOW)

- 1 teaspoon salt, plus additional for seasoning
- ½ teaspoon black pepper, plus additional for seasoning
- 1 butternut squash (about 2 pounds), peeled and seeded
- 2 apples, cored and cut into slices
- 1 medium onion, quartered and sliced
- 1½ tablespoons butter

1. Combine salt and pepper in small bowl; set aside.

2. Cut squash into 2-inch pieces; place in **CROCK·POT**® slow cooker. Add apples and onion. Sprinkle with salt mixture; stir well. Cover; cook on LOW 6 to 7 hours or until vegetables are tender.

3. Just before serving, stir in butter and season with additional salt and pepper, if desired.

Variation: Add ¼ to ½ cup brown sugar and ½ teaspoon ground cinnamon along with butter; mix well.

Wild Rice and Mushroom Casserole

MAKES 4 TO 6 SERVINGS

PREP TIME: 10 TO 15 MINUTES

COOK TIME: 4 TO 6 HOURS (LOW) ■ 2 TO 3 HOURS (HIGH)

- 2 tablespoons olive oil
- ½ medium red onion, finely diced
- 1 large green bell pepper, finely diced
- 8 ounces button mushrooms, thinly sliced
- 2 cloves garlic, minced
- 1 can (14 ounces) diced tomatoes, drained
- 1 teaspoon dried oregano
- 1 teaspoon paprika
- 2 tablespoons butter
- 2 tablespoons all-purpose flour
- 1½ cups milk
- 8 ounces pepper-jack, Cheddar or Swiss cheese, shredded
- 1 teaspoon salt
- ½ teaspoon black pepper
- 2 cups wild rice, cooked according to package instructions

1. Coat **CROCK-POT**® slow cooker with nonstick cooking spray.

2. Heat oil in large skillet over medium heat until hot. Add onion, bell pepper and mushrooms. Cook and stir 5 to 6 minutes or until vegetables soften. Add garlic, tomatoes, oregano and paprika. Continue to cook and stir until heated through. Transfer to large mixing bowl to cool.

3. Melt butter in same skillet over medium heat; whisk in flour. Cook and stir until smooth and golden, about 4 to 5 minutes. Whisk in milk and bring to a boil. Whisk shredded cheese into boiling milk, stirring to produce rich, velvety sauce.

4. Combine cooked wild rice with vegetables in large mixing bowl. Fold in cheese sauce and mix gently. Pour into **CROCK-POT**® slow cooker. Cover; cook on LOW 4 to 6 hours or on HIGH 2 to 3 hours or until done.

Sweet Endings

FRESH, TASTY DESSERTS FOR THE PERFECT FINISH

Cherry Flan

MAKES 6 SERVINGS

PREP TIME: 10 MINUTES

COOK TIME: 3½ TO 4 HOURS (LOW)

5	eggs
½	cup sugar
½	teaspoon salt
¾	cup all-purpose flour
1	can (12 ounces) evaporated milk
1	teaspoon vanilla
1	bag (16 ounces) frozen pitted, dark sweet cherries, thawed
	Whipped cream or cherry vanilla ice cream

1. Coat **CROCK-POT**® slow cooker with butter or nonstick cooking spray.

2. Beat eggs, sugar and salt in large bowl with electric mixer at high speed until thick and pale yellow. Add flour; beat until smooth. Beat in evaporated milk and vanilla.

3. Pour batter into **CROCK-POT**® slow cooker. Place cherries evenly over batter. Cover; cook on LOW 3½ to 4 hours or until flan is set. Serve warm with whipped cream.

Decadent Chocolate Delight

MAKES 12 SERVINGS

PREP TIME: 5 TO 10 MINUTES

COOK TIME: 3 TO 4 HOURS (LOW) ■ 1½ TO 1¾ HOURS (HIGH)

- 1 package (about 18 ounces) chocolate cake mix
- 1 container (8 ounces) sour cream
- 1 cup semisweet chocolate chips
- 1 cup water
- 4 eggs
- ¾ cup vegetable oil
- 1 package (4-serving size) instant chocolate pudding and pie filling mix

1. Coat **CROCK-POT**® slow cooker with butter or nonstick cooking spray.

2. Combine all ingredients in medium bowl; mix well. Transfer to **CROCK-POT**® slow cooker.

3. Cover; cook on LOW 3 to 4 hours or on HIGH 1½ to 1¾ hours. Serve hot or warm with ice cream.

HELPFUL HINTS

Keep these general guidelines in mind when making delicious desserts and baked goods in your **CROCK-POT**® slow cooker:

- Do not overbeat cake and bread batters. Follow all recommended mixing times.

- Do not add water to the **CROCK-POT**® slow cooker unless instructed to do so in the recipe.

- After cakes and breads have finished cooking, allow them to cool in the stoneware at least 5 minutes before removing.

Peach Cobbler

MAKES 4 TO 6 SERVINGS

PREP TIME: 10 MINUTES

COOK TIME: 2 HOURS (HIGH)

- 2 packages (16 ounces each) frozen peaches, thawed and drained
- ¾ cup plus 1 tablespoon sugar, divided
- 2 teaspoons ground cinnamon, divided
- ½ teaspoon ground nutmeg
- ¾ cup all-purpose flour
- 6 tablespoons butter, cut into small pieces
- Whipped cream (optional)

1. Combine peaches, ¾ cup sugar, 1½ teaspoons cinnamon and nutmeg in medium bowl. Transfer to **CROCK·POT®** slow cooker.

2. For topping: Combine flour, remaining 1 tablespoon sugar and remaining ½ teaspoon cinnamon in small bowl. Cut in butter with pastry blender or 2 knives until mixture resembles coarse crumbs. Sprinkle over peach mixture. Cover; cook on HIGH 2 hours. Serve with whipped cream, if desired.

Strawberry Rhubarb Crisp

MAKES 8 SERVINGS

PREP TIME: 20 MINUTES

COOK TIME: 1½ HOURS (HIGH) PLUS 15 TO 20 MINUTES (375°F OVEN)

FRUIT FILLING
- 4 cups sliced hulled strawberries
- 4 cups diced rhubarb (about 5 stalks), cut into ½-inch dice
- 1½ cups granulated sugar
- 2 tablespoons lemon juice
- 1½ tablespoons cornstarch, plus water (optional)

TOPPING
- 1 cup all-purpose flour
- 1 cup old-fashioned oats
- ½ cup granulated sugar
- ½ cup packed brown sugar
- ½ teaspoon ground ginger
- ½ teaspoon ground nutmeg
- ½ cup (1 stick) butter, cut into small pieces
- ½ cup sliced almonds, toasted*

*To toast almonds, spread in single layer in heavy-bottomed skillet. Cook over medium heat 1 to 2 minutes, stirring frequently, until nuts are lightly browned. Remove from skillet immediately. Cool before using.

1. For fruit filling: Coat **CROCK-POT**® slow cooker with butter or nonstick cooking spray. Place strawberries, rhubarb, sugar and lemon juice in **CROCK-POT**® slow cooker; mix well. Cover; cook on HIGH 1½ hours or until fruit is tender.

2. If fruit is dry, add a little water. If fruit has too much liquid, mix cornstarch with a small amount of water and stir into fruit. Cook on HIGH 15 minutes longer or until cooking liquid has thickened.

3. For topping: Preheat oven to 375°F. Combine flour, oats, sugars, ginger and nutmeg in medium bowl. Cut in butter using pastry blender or 2 knives until mixture resembles small peas. Stir in almonds.

4. Remove lid from **CROCK-POT**® slow cooker; gently sprinkle topping on fruit. Transfer stoneware to oven. Bake 15 to 20 minutes or until topping begins to brown.

Brownie Bottoms

MAKES 6 SERVINGS

PREP TIME: 12 MINUTES

COOK TIME: 1½ HOURS (HIGH)

- ¾ cup water
- ½ cup brown sugar
- 2 tablespoons unsweetened cocoa powder
- 2½ cups packaged brownie mix
- 1 package (2¾ ounces) instant chocolate pudding mix
- ½ cup milk chocolate chips
- 2 eggs, beaten
- 3 tablespoons butter or margarine, melted
    Whipped cream or ice cream (optional)

1. Lightly coat **CROCK-POT**® slow cooker with butter or nonstick cooking spray. Combine water, brown sugar and cocoa powder in small saucepan; bring to a boil.

2. Combine brownie mix, pudding mix, chocolate chips, eggs and butter in medium bowl; stir until well blended. Spread batter into **CROCK-POT**®

slow cooker. Pour boiling mixture over batter. *Do not stir.* Cover; cook on HIGH 1 ½ hours.

3. Turn off **CROCK-POT**® slow cooker and let stand 30 minutes. Serve warm with whipped cream, if desired.

Tip: For a 5-, 6- or 7-quart **CROCK-POT**® slow cooker, you may double all ingredients.

Apple-Date Crisp

MAKES 6 SERVINGS

PREP TIME: 20 TO 30 MINUTES

COOK TIME: 4 HOURS (LOW) ■ 2 HOURS (HIGH)

- 6 cups thinly sliced peeled apples (about 6 medium apples, preferably Golden Delicious)
- 2 teaspoons lemon juice
- ⅓ cup chopped dates
- 1⅓ cups uncooked quick oats
- ½ cup all-purpose flour
- ½ cup packed light brown sugar
- ½ teaspoon ground cinnamon
- ¼ teaspoon ground ginger
- ¼ teaspoon salt
  Dash ground nutmeg
  Dash ground cloves (optional)
- 4 tablespoons (½ stick) cold butter, cut into small pieces

1. Coat **CROCK-POT**® slow cooker with butter or nonstick cooking spray. Place apples in medium bowl. Sprinkle with lemon juice; toss to coat. Add dates and mix well. Transfer to **CROCK-POT**® slow cooker.

2. For topping: Combine oats, flour, brown sugar, cinnamon, ginger, salt, nutmeg and cloves, if desired, in medium bowl. Cut in butter with pastry blender or 2 knives until mixture resembles coarse crumbs.

3. Sprinkle oat mixture over apples; smooth top. Cover; cook on LOW about 4 hours or on HIGH about 2 hours, or until apples are tender.

"Peachy Keen" Dessert Treat

MAKES 8 TO 12 SERVINGS

PREP TIME: 10 TO 15 MINUTES

COOK TIME: 4 TO 6 HOURS (LOW)

- 1⅓ cups uncooked old-fashioned oats
- 1 cup granulated sugar
- 1 cup packed light brown sugar
- ⅔ cup buttermilk baking mix
- 2 teaspoons ground cinnamon
- ½ teaspoon ground nutmeg
- 2 pounds fresh peaches (about 8 medium), sliced

Coat **CROCK-POT**® slow cooker with nonstick cooking spray. Combine oats, sugars, baking mix, cinnamon and nutmeg in large bowl. Stir in peaches until well blended. Transfer to **CROCK-POT**® slow cooker. Cover; cook on LOW 4 to 6 hours or until done.

Streusel Pound Cake

MAKES 6 TO 8 SERVINGS

PREP TIME: 10 TO 15 MINUTES

COOK TIME: 1½ TO 1¾ HOURS (HIGH)

- 1 package (16 ounces) pound cake mix, plus ingredients to prepare mix
- ¼ cup packed light brown sugar
- 1 tablespoon all-purpose flour
- ¼ cup chopped nuts
- 1 teaspoon ground cinnamon

Coat **CROCK-POT**® slow cooker with nonstick cooking spray. Prepare cake mix according to package directions; stir in brown sugar, flour, nuts and cinnamon. Pour batter into **CROCK-POT**® slow cooker. Cover; cook on HIGH 1½ to 1¾ hours or until toothpick inserted into center of cake comes out clean.

Coconut Rice Pudding

MAKES 6 SERVINGS

PREP TIME: 30 TO 35 MINUTES

COOK TIME: 4 HOURS (LOW) ■ 2 HOURS (HIGH)

- 2 cups water
- 1 cup uncooked converted long-grain rice
- 1 tablespoon unsalted butter
  Pinch salt
- 2¼ cups evaporated milk
- 1 can (14 ounces) cream of coconut
- ½ cup golden raisins
- 3 egg yolks, beaten
  Grated peel of 2 limes
- 1 teaspoon vanilla
  Toasted shredded coconut (optional)

1. Place water, rice, butter and salt in medium saucepan. Bring to rolling boil over high heat, stirring frequently. Reduce heat to low. Cover; cook 10 to 12 minutes. Remove from heat. Let stand, covered, 5 minutes.

2. Coat **CROCK-POT**® slow cooker with nonstick cooking spray. Add evaporated milk, cream of coconut, raisins, egg yolks, lime peel and vanilla; mix well. Add rice; stir until blended.

3. Cover; cook on LOW 4 hours or on HIGH 2 hours. Stir every 30 minutes, if possible. Pudding will thicken as it cools. Top with toasted coconut, if desired.

Bananas Foster

MAKES 12 SERVINGS

PREP TIME: 5 TO 10 MINUTES

COOK TIME: 1 TO 2 HOURS (LOW)

12	bananas, cut into quarters
1	cup flaked coconut
1	teaspoon ground cinnamon
½	teaspoon salt
1	cup dark corn syrup
⅔	cup butter, melted
2	teaspoons grated lemon peel
¼	cup lemon juice
2	teaspoons rum
12	slices pound cake
1	quart vanilla ice cream

Combine bananas and coconut in **CROCK-POT**® slow cooker. Combine cinnamon, salt, corn syrup, butter, lemon peel, lemon juice and rum in medium bowl; pour over bananas. Cover; cook on LOW 1 to 2 hours. To serve, arrange bananas on pound cake slices. Top with ice cream and pour on warm sauce.

Baked Ginger Apples

MAKES 4 SERVINGS

PREP TIME: 10 TO 15 MINUTES

COOK TIME: 4½ HOURS (LOW) ■ 2½ HOURS (HIGH)

4	large Red Delicious apples
½	cup (1 stick) unsalted butter, melted
⅓	cup chopped macadamia nuts
¼	cup chopped dried apricots
2	tablespoons finely chopped crystallized ginger
1	tablespoon packed dark brown sugar
¾	cup brandy
½	cup vanilla pudding and pie filling mix
2	cups heavy cream

1. Slice tops off apples; remove cores. Combine butter, nuts, apricots, ginger and brown sugar in medium bowl. Fill apples with nut mixture. Transfer to **CROCK-POT**® slow cooker. Pour brandy over apples. Cover; cook on LOW 4 hours or on HIGH 2 hours.

2. Gently remove apples from **CROCK-POT**® slow cooker with slotted spoon; keep warm. Combine pudding mix and cream in small bowl. Add to cooking liquid in **CROCK-POT**® slow cooker; stir well. Turn heat up to HIGH. Cover; cook on HIGH 30 minutes. Stir until smooth. Return apples to **CROCK-POT**® slow cooker; keep warm until ready to serve with warm cream sauce.

Gingerbread

MAKES 6 TO 8 SERVINGS

PREP TIME: 10 TO 15 MINUTES

COOK TIME: 1½ TO 1¾ HOURS (HIGH)

½ cup butter, softened
½ cup sugar
1 egg, lightly beaten
1 cup light molasses
2½ cups all-purpose flour
1½ teaspoons baking soda
1 teaspoon ground cinnamon
2 teaspoons ground ginger
½ teaspoon ground cloves
½ teaspoon salt
1 cup hot water
Whipped cream, optional

1. Coat **CROCK-POT**® slow cooker with butter or nonstick cooking spray. Beat butter and sugar in large bowl. Add egg, molasses, flour, baking soda, cinnamon, ginger, cloves and salt. Stir in hot water and mix well. Pour batter into **CROCK-POT**® slow cooker.

2. Cover; cook on HIGH 1½ to 1¾ hours or until toothpick inserted in center of cake comes out clean. Serve warm; top with whipped cream, if desired.

Everyday Favorites

FAST, FAMILY-PLEASING RECIPES FOR EVERY MEAL

Scalloped Potatoes & Ham

MAKES 5 TO 6 SERVINGS

PREP TIME: 10 MINUTES

COOK TIME: 3½ HOURS (HIGH) PLUS 1 HOUR (LOW)

6 large russet potatoes, sliced into ¼-inch rounds
1 ham steak (about 1½ pounds), cut into cubes
1 can (10¾ ounces) condensed cream of mushroom soup
1 soup can water
1 cup shredded Cheddar cheese
Grill seasoning, to taste

1. Layer potatoes and ham in **CROCK-POT**® slow cooker.

2. Combine soup, water, cheese and seasoning in large mixing bowl. Pour mixture over potatoes and ham.

3. Cover and cook on HIGH 3½ hours until potatoes are fork-tender. Turn **CROCK-POT**® slow cooker to LOW and continue cooking 1 hour.

Chicken Fiesta Soup

MAKES 8 SERVINGS

PREP TIME: 15 MINUTES

COOK TIME: 8 HOURS (LOW)

- 4 boneless skinless cooked chicken breasts, shredded
- 1 can (14½ ounces) stewed tomatoes, drained
- 2 cans (4 ounces each) chopped green chilies
- 1 can (28 ounces) enchilada sauce
- 1 can (14½ ounces) chicken broth
- 1 cup finely chopped onion
- 2 cloves garlic, minced
- 1 teaspoon ground cumin
- 1 teaspoon chili powder
- ¾ teaspoon pepper
- 1 teaspoon salt
- ¼ cup minced fresh cilantro
- 1 cup frozen whole kernel corn
- 1 yellow squash, diced
- 1 zucchini, diced
- 8 tostada shells, crumbled
- 8 ounces shredded Cheddar cheese

1. Combine chicken, tomatoes, chilies, enchilada sauce, broth, onions, garlic, cumin, chili powder, pepper, salt, cilantro, corn, squash and zucchini in **CROCK·POT**® slow cooker.

2. Cover and cook on LOW 8 hours. To serve, fill individual bowls with soup. Garnish with crumbled tostada shells and cheese.

Mexican Cheese Soup

MAKES 6 TO 8 SERVINGS

PREP TIME: 20 TO 25 MINUTES

COOK TIME: 4 TO 5 HOURS (LOW) ■ 3 HOURS (HIGH)

1 pound processed cheese, cubed
1 pound ground beef, cooked and drained
1 can (8¾ ounces) whole kernel corn, undrained
1 can (15 ounces) kidney beans, undrained
1 jalapeño pepper, seeded and diced* (optional)
1 can (14½ ounces) diced tomatoes with green chilies, undrained
1 can (14½ ounces) stewed tomatoes, undrained
1 envelope taco seasoning

*Jalapeño peppers can sting and irritate the skin; wear rubber gloves when handling peppers and do not touch eyes. Wash hands after handling.

1. Coat **CROCK-POT**® slow cooker with nonstick cooking spray. Combine cheese, beef, corn, beans, jalapeño, if desired, tomatoes with chilies and stewed tomatoes in **CROCK-POT**® slow cooker.

2. Cover; cook on LOW for 4 to 5 hours or on HIGH for 3 hours or until done. Serve with corn chips, if desired.

Three-Bean Turkey Chili

MAKES 6 TO 8 SERVINGS

PREP TIME: 10 TO 15 MINUTES

COOK TIME: 6 TO 8 HOURS (HIGH)

1   pound ground turkey
1   small onion, chopped
1   can (28 ounces) diced tomatoes, undrained
1   can (15 ounces) chickpeas, rinsed and drained
1   can (15 ounces) kidney beans, rinsed and drained
1   can (15 ounces) black beans, rinsed and drained
1   can (8 ounces) tomato sauce
1   can (4 ounces) chopped mild green chilies
1   to 2 tablespoons chili powder

1. Cook and stir turkey and onion in medium skillet over medium-high heat until turkey is no longer pink. Drain and discard fat. Transfer to **CROCK-POT**® slow cooker.

2. Add tomatoes with juice, beans, tomato sauce, chilies and chili powder; mix well. Cover; cook on HIGH 6 to 8 hours or until done.

Super Slow Sloppy Joes

MAKES 8 SERVINGS

PREP TIME: 15 TO 20 MINUTES

COOK TIME: 6 TO 8 HOURS (LOW)

- 3 pounds 90% lean ground beef
- 1 cup chopped onion
- 3 cloves garlic, minced
- 1¼ cups ketchup
- 1 cup chopped red bell pepper
- 5 tablespoons Worcestershire sauce
- ¼ cup packed brown sugar
- 3 tablespoons vinegar
- 3 tablespoons prepared mustard
- 2 teaspoons chili powder
  Hamburger buns

1. Brown ground beef, onion and garlic in large nonstick skillet over medium-high heat in 2 batches, stirring to separate meat. Drain and discard fat.

2. Combine ketchup, bell pepper, Worcestershire sauce, brown sugar, vinegar, mustard and chili powder in **CROCK-POT**® slow cooker. Stir in beef mixture.

3. Cover; cook on LOW 6 to 8 hours or until done. Spoon onto hamburger buns.

Barbecued Pulled Pork Sandwiches

MAKES 8 SERVINGS

PREP TIME: 15 TO 20 MINUTES

COOK TIME: 12 TO 14 HOURS (LOW) ■ 6 TO 7 HOURS (HIGH)

- 1 pork shoulder roast (about 2½ pounds)
- 1 bottle (14 ounces) barbecue sauce
- 1 tablespoon fresh lemon juice
- 1 teaspoon brown sugar
- 1 medium onion, chopped
- 8 hamburger buns or hard rolls

1. Place pork roast in **CROCK-POT**® slow cooker. Cover; cook on LOW 10 to 12 hours or on HIGH 5 to 6 hours or until done.

2. Remove pork roast from **CROCK-POT**® slow cooker; discard cooking liquid. Shred pork with 2 forks. Return pork to **CROCK-POT**® slow cooker. Add barbecue sauce, lemon juice, brown sugar and onion. Cover and cook on LOW 2 hours or on HIGH 1 hour.

3. Serve shredded pork on hamburger buns or hard rolls.

Note: For a 5-, 6- or 7-quart **CROCK-POT**® slow cooker, double all ingredients, except barbecue sauce. Increase barbecue sauce to 21 ounces.

Classic Spaghetti

MAKES 6 TO 8 SERVINGS

PREP TIME: 20 TO 30 MINUTES

COOK TIME: 6 TO 8 HOURS (LOW) ■ 3 TO 5 HOURS (HIGH)

- 2 tablespoons olive oil
- 2 onions, chopped
- 2 green bell peppers, sliced
- 2 stalks celery, sliced
- 4 teaspoons minced garlic
- 3 pounds lean ground beef
- 2 carrots, diced
- 1 cup sliced mushrooms
- 1 can (28 ounces) tomato sauce
- 1 can (28 ounces) stewed tomatoes, undrained
- 3 cups water
- 2 tablespoons minced parsley
- 1 tablespoon dried oregano
- 1 tablespoon sugar
- 2 teaspoons salt
- 2 teaspoons black pepper
- 1 pound dry spaghetti

1. Heat oil in large skillet over medium-high heat until hot. Add onion, bell pepper, celery and garlic; cook and stir until tender. Transfer to **CROCK-POT**® slow cooker.

2. In same skillet, brown ground beef. Drain and discard fat. Add beef, carrots, mushrooms, tomato sauce, tomatoes with juice, water, parsley, oregano, sugar, salt and black pepper to **CROCK-POT**® slow cooker. Cover; cook on LOW 6 to 8 hours or on HIGH 3 to 5 hours or until done.

3. Cook spaghetti according to package directions; drain. Serve sauce over cooked spaghetti.

Hot & Juicy Reuben Sandwiches

MAKES 4 SERVINGS

PREP TIME: 25 MINUTES

COOK TIME: 7 TO 9 HOURS (LOW)

- 1   mild-cure corned beef (about 1½ pounds)
- 2   cups sauerkraut, drained
- ½   cup beef broth
- 1   small onion, sliced
- 1   clove garlic, minced
- ¼   teaspoon caraway seeds
- 4   to 6 peppercorns
- 8   slices pumpernickel or rye bread
- 4   slices Swiss cheese
-     Mustard

1. Trim and discard excess fat from corned beef. Place beef in **CROCK-POT**® slow cooker. Add sauerkraut, broth, onion, garlic, caraway seeds and peppercorns. Cover; cook on LOW 7 to 9 hours.

2. Remove beef from **CROCK-POT**® slow cooker. Cut across grain into 4 (½-inch-thick) slices. Divide evenly among 4 slices bread. Top each slice with ½ cup drained sauerkraut mixture and 1 slice cheese. Spread mustard on remaining 4 bread slices and place on sandwiches.

Philly Cheese Steaks

MAKES 8 SERVINGS

PREP TIME: 10 TO 15 MINUTES

COOK TIME: 6 TO 8 HOURS (LOW)

- 2 pounds round steak, sliced
- 2 tablespoons butter or margarine, melted
- 4 onions, sliced
- 2 green bell peppers, sliced
- 1 tablespoon garlic-pepper blend
  Salt, to taste
- ½ cup water
- 2 teaspoons beef bouillon granules
- 8 crusty Italian or French rolls*
- 8 slices Cheddar cheese, cut into halves

*Toast rolls on griddle or under broiler, if desired.

1. Combine steak, butter, onions, bell peppers, garlic-pepper blend and salt in **CROCK-POT**® slow cooker; stir to mix.

2. Whisk together water and bouillon in small bowl; pour into **CROCK-POT**® slow cooker. Cover; cook on LOW 6 to 8 hours.

3. Remove meat, onions and bell peppers from **CROCK-POT**® slow cooker and pile on rolls. Top with cheese and place under broiler until cheese is melted.

Simple Turkey Soup

MAKES 8 SERVINGS

PREP TIME: 10 TO 15 MINUTES

COOK TIME: 3 TO 4 HOURS (HIGH)

- 2 pounds ground turkey, cooked and drained
- 1 can (28 ounces) whole tomatoes, undrained
- 2 cans (14 ounces each) beef broth
- 1 bag (16 ounces) frozen mixed soup vegetables
- ½ cup uncooked barley
- 1 teaspoon salt
- 1 teaspoon dried thyme
- ½ teaspoon ground coriander
  Dash black pepper

1. Combine turkey, tomatoes with juice, broth, vegetables, barley, salt, thyme, coriander and pepper in **CROCK-POT®** slow cooker. Add water to cover.

2. Cover; cook on HIGH 3 to 4 hours or until barley and vegetables are tender.

Oriental Chicken Wings

MAKES 32 APPETIZERS

PREP TIME: 15 TO 20 MINUTES

COOK TIME: 5 TO 6 HOURS (LOW) ■ 2 TO 3 HOURS (HIGH)

16	chicken wings, split and tips removed
1	cup chopped red onion
1	cup soy sauce
¾	cup packed light brown sugar
¼	cup dry cooking sherry
2	tablespoons chopped fresh ginger
2	cloves garlic, minced
	Chopped fresh chives

1. Preheat broiler. Broil chicken wings about 5 minutes per side. Transfer to **CROCK-POT**® slow cooker.

2. Combine onion, soy sauce, brown sugar, sherry, ginger and garlic in large bowl. Add to **CROCK-POT**® slow cooker; stir to blend well.

3. Cover; cook on LOW 5 to 6 hours or on HIGH 2 to 3 hours. Sprinkle with chives before serving.

Kids in the Kitchen

EASY HANDS-ON RECIPES FOR ASPIRING YOUNG CHEFS

Mom's Tuna Casserole

MAKES 8 SERVINGS

PREP TIME: 10 MINUTES

COOK TIME: 5 TO 8 HOURS (LOW)

2   cans (12 ounces each) tuna, drained and flaked
3   cups diced celery
3   cups crushed potato chips, divided
6   hard-cooked eggs, chopped
1   can (10¾ ounces) condensed cream of mushroom soup
1   can (10¾ ounces) condensed cream of celery soup
1   cup mayonnaise
1   teaspoon dried tarragon
1   teaspoon black pepper

1. Combine tuna, celery, 2½ cups chips, eggs, soups, mayonnaise, tarragon and pepper in **CROCK-POT**® slow cooker; stir well.

2. Cover; cook on LOW 5 to 8 hours or until done.

3. Sprinkle with remaining ½ cup chips before serving.

Macaroni and Cheese

MAKES 6 TO 8 SERVINGS

PREP TIME: 10 TO 15 MINUTES

COOK TIME: 2 TO 3 HOURS (HIGH)

- 6 cups cooked macaroni
- 2 tablespoons butter
- 4 cups evaporated milk
- 6 cups Cheddar cheese, shredded
- 2 teaspoons salt
- ½ teaspoon black pepper

In large mixing bowl, toss macaroni with butter. Stir in evaporated milk, cheese, salt and pepper; place in **CROCK-POT**® slow cooker. Cover; cook on HIGH 2 to 3 hours.

Easiest Chicken & Biscuits

MAKES 4 SERVINGS

PREP TIME: 10 MINUTES

COOK TIME: 4 TO 6 HOURS (LOW)

- 2 cups cooked chicken, cubed
- 1 can (10¾ ounces) condensed cream of mushroom soup
- 1 can (10¾ ounces) condensed cream of chicken soup
- 1½ to 2 soup cans water
- 2 teaspoons chicken bouillon granules
- ½ teaspoon black pepper
- 1 container (8-pack) refrigerated buttermilk biscuits

Combine chicken, soups, water, bouillon and pepper in **CROCK-POT**® slow cooker. Cut biscuits into quarters; gently stir into mixture. Cover; cook on LOW for 4 to 6 hours, stirring occasionally, or until done.

Triple Chocolate Fantasy

MAKES 36 SERVINGS

PREP TIME: 20 MINUTES

COOK TIME: 1 HOUR (HIGH) PLUS 1 HOUR (LOW)

2   pounds white almond bark, broken into pieces
1   bar (4 ounces) German chocolate, broken into pieces
1   package (12 ounces) semisweet chocolate chips
3   cups lightly toasted, coarsely chopped pecans

1. Place chocolates in **CROCK-POT**® slow cooker. Cover; cook on HIGH 1 hour. *Do not stir.*

2. Turn **CROCK-POT**® slow cooker to LOW. Continue cooking 1 hour, stirring every 15 minutes. Stir in nuts.

3. Drop mixture by tablespoonfuls onto baking sheet covered with waxed paper; let cool. Store in tightly covered container.

Variations: Here are a few ideas for other imaginative add-ins:

- raisins
- chopped gum drops
- crushed peppermint candy
- chopped dried fruit
- candy-coated baking bits

- candied cherries
- crushed toffee
- chopped marshmallows
- peanuts or pistachios
- sweetened coconut

Chunky Sweet Spiced Apple Butter

MAKES 2 CUPS

PREP TIME: 15 MINUTES

COOK TIME: 8 HOURS (LOW)

- **4** cups peeled chopped Granny Smith apples (about 1¼ pounds)
- **¾** cup packed dark brown sugar
- **2** tablespoons balsamic vinegar
- **4** tablespoons (½ stick) butter, divided
- **1** tablespoon ground cinnamon
- **½** teaspoon salt
- **¼** teaspoon ground cloves
- **1½** teaspoons vanilla

Combine apples, sugar, vinegar, 2 tablespoons butter, cinnamon, salt and cloves in **CROCK-POT**® slow cooker. Cover; cook on LOW 8 hours. Stir in remaining 2 tablespoons butter and vanilla. Cool completely.

Sweet & Saucy Ribs

MAKES 4 SERVINGS

PREP TIME: 20 TO 25 MINUTES

COOK TIME: 6 TO 8 HOURS (LOW) ■ 3 TO 4 HOURS (HIGH)

- 2 pounds pork baby back ribs
- 1 teaspoon black pepper
- 2½ cups barbecue sauce (not mesquite-flavored)
- 1 jar (8 ounces) cherry jam or preserves
- 1 tablespoon Dijon mustard
- ¼ teaspoon salt
  Salt and black pepper, to taste

1. Trim and discard excess fat from ribs. Rub 1 teaspoon black pepper over ribs. Cut ribs into 2-rib portions; place in **CROCK-POT**® slow cooker.

2. Combine barbecue sauce, jam, mustard and ¼ teaspoon salt in small bowl; pour over ribs. Cover; cook on LOW 6 to 8 hours or HIGH 3 to 4 hours, or until ribs are tender.

3. Taste and adjust seasonings with additional salt and pepper, if desired. Serve ribs with sauce.

Pumpkin-Cranberry Custard

MAKES 4 TO 6 SERVINGS

PREP TIME: 10 MINUTES

COOK TIME: 4 TO 4½ HOURS (HIGH)

1   can (30 ounces) pumpkin pie filling
1   can (12 ounces) evaporated milk
1   cup dried cranberries
4   eggs, beaten
1   cup crushed or whole gingersnap cookies (optional)
    Whipped cream (optional)

Combine pumpkin, evaporated milk, cranberries and eggs in **CROCK-POT**®
slow cooker; mix thoroughly. Cover; cook on HIGH 4 to 4½ hours or until
done. Serve with whole or crushed gingersnaps and whipped cream, if
desired.

slow cooker Steak Fajitas

MAKES 4 SERVINGS

PREP TIME: 20 MINUTES

COOK TIME: 6 TO 7 HOURS (LOW)

- **1** beef flank steak (about 1 pound)
- **1** medium onion, cut into strips
- **½** cup medium salsa, plus additional for garnish
- **2** tablespoons fresh lime juice
- **2** tablespoons chopped fresh cilantro
- **2** cloves garlic, minced
- **1** tablespoon chili powder
- **1** teaspoon ground cumin
- **½** teaspoon salt
- **1** small green bell pepper, cut into strips
- **1** small red bell pepper, cut into strips
  Flour tortillas, warmed

1. Cut flank steak lengthwise in half, then crosswise into thin strips. Combine onion, ½ cup salsa, lime juice, cilantro, garlic, chili powder, cumin and salt in **CROCK-POT**® slow cooker. Add steak and stir well. Cover; cook on LOW 5 to 6 hours.

2. Add bell peppers. Cover; cook on LOW 1 hour.

3. Serve with flour tortillas and additional salsa, if desired.

Three-Cheese Chicken & Noodles

MAKES 6 SERVINGS

PREP TIME: 10 MINUTES

COOK TIME: 6 TO 10 HOURS (LOW) ■ 3 TO 4 HOURS (HIGH)

- 3 cups chopped cooked chicken
- 1½ cups cottage cheese
- 1 can (10¾ ounces) condensed cream of chicken soup
- 1 package (8 ounces) wide egg noodles, cooked and drained
- 1 cup diced green and/or red bell pepper
- 1 cup grated Monterey Jack cheese
- ½ cup grated Parmesan cheese
- ½ cup diced celery
- ½ cup diced onion
- ½ cup chicken broth
- 1 can (4 ounces) sliced mushrooms, drained
- 2 tablespoons butter, melted
- ½ teaspoon dried thyme

Combine all ingredients in **CROCK-POT**® slow cooker. Stir to coat evenly. Cover; cook on LOW 6 to 10 hours or on HIGH 3 to 4 hours.

Southwestern Stuffed Peppers

MAKES 4 SERVINGS

PREP TIME: 15 MINUTES

COOK TIME: 4 TO 6 HOURS (LOW)

- **4** green and/or red peppers
- **1** can (15 ounces) black beans, rinsed and drained
- **1** cup (4 ounces) shredded pepper-jack cheese
- **¾** cup medium salsa
- **½** cup frozen whole kernel corn, thawed
- **½** cup chopped green onions with tops
- **⅓** cup uncooked long-grain converted rice
- **1** teaspoon chili powder
- **½** teaspoon ground cumin
  Sour cream (optional)

1. Cut thin slice off top of each bell pepper. Carefully remove seeds, leaving pepper whole.

2. Combine beans, cheese, salsa, corn, onions, rice, chili powder and cumin in medium bowl. Spoon filling evenly into each pepper. Place in **CROCK-POT**® slow cooker.

3. Cover; cook on LOW 4 to 6 hours. Serve with sour cream, if desired.

Triple Delicious Hot Chocolate

MAKES 6 SERVINGS

PREP TIME: 10 MINUTES

COOK TIME: 2¼ HOURS (LOW)

- ⅓ **cup sugar**
- ¼ **cup unsweetened cocoa powder**
- ¼ **teaspoon salt**
- 3 **cups milk, divided**
- ¾ **teaspoon vanilla**
- 1 **cup heavy cream**
- 1 **square (1 ounce) bittersweet chocolate**
- 1 **square (1 ounce) white chocolate**
- ¾ **cup whipped cream**
- 6 **teaspoons mini chocolate chips or shaved bittersweet chocolate**

1. Combine sugar, cocoa, salt and ½ cup milk in medium bowl. Beat until smooth. Pour into **CROCK-POT**® slow cooker. Add remaining 2½ cups milk and vanilla. Cover; cook on LOW 2 hours.

2. Add cream. Cover; cook on LOW 10 to 15 minutes. Stir in bittersweet and white chocolates until melted.

3. Pour hot chocolate into 6 cups. Top each with 2 tablespoons whipped cream and 1 teaspoon chocolate chips.

Index

METRIC CONVERSION CHART

VOLUME MEASUREMENTS (dry)

1/8 teaspoon = 0.5 mL
1/4 teaspoon = 1 mL
1/2 teaspoon = 2 mL
3/4 teaspoon = 4 mL
1 teaspoon = 5 mL
1 tablespoon = 15 mL
2 tablespoons = 30 mL
1/4 cup = 60 mL
1/3 cup = 75 mL
1/2 cup = 125 mL
2/3 cup = 150 mL
3/4 cup = 175 mL
1 cup = 250 mL
2 cups = 1 pint = 500 mL
3 cups = 750 mL
4 cups = 1 quart = 1 L

VOLUME MEASUREMENTS (fluid)

1 fluid ounce (2 tablespoons) = 30 mL
4 fluid ounces (1/2 cup) = 125 mL
8 fluid ounces (1 cup) = 250 mL
12 fluid ounces (1 1/2 cups) = 375 mL
16 fluid ounces (2 cups) = 500 mL

WEIGHTS (mass)

1/2 ounce = 15 g
1 ounce = 30 g
3 ounces = 90 g
4 ounces = 120 g
8 ounces = 225 g
10 ounces = 285 g
12 ounces = 360 g
16 ounces = 1 pound = 450 g

DIMENSIONS

1/16 inch = 2 mm
1/8 inch = 3 mm
1/4 inch = 6 mm
1/2 inch = 1.5 cm
3/4 inch = 2 cm
1 inch = 2.5 cm

OVEN TEMPERATURES

250°F = 120°C
275°F = 140°C
300°F = 150°C
325°F = 160°C
350°F = 180°C
375°F = 190°C
400°F = 200°C
425°F = 220°C
450°F = 230°C

BAKING PAN SIZES

Utensil	Size in Inches/Quarts	Metric Volume	Size in Centimeters
Baking or Cake Pan (square or rectangular)	8×8×2	2 L	20×20×5
	9×9×2	2.5 L	23×23×5
	12×8×2	3 L	30×20×5
	13×9×2	3.5 L	33×23×5
Loaf Pan	8×4×3	1.5 L	20×10×7
	9×5×3	2 L	23×13×7
Round Layer Cake Pan	8×1½	1.2 L	20×4
	9×1½	1.5 L	23×4
Pie Plate	8×1¼	750 mL	20×3
	9×1¼	1 L	23×3
Baking Dish or Casserole	1 quart	1 L	—
	1½ quart	1.5 L	—
	2 quart	2 L	—

Notes